Join Us at the Table

Iraqi Kurds

Part of the
"Preserving Heritage through Cooking"
recipe book series.

The series takes you to conflict ridden corners of the globe where people face the challenge of feeding their families. Explore their ingenuity and stalwart perseverance as they join at the table and pass their histories and customs to the rising generation.

www.heritagethrucooking.com

Published By
The Jones Kilmartin Group, LLC
www.joneskilmartingroup.com

Design and Editing
Jordan Loria

Photography
Erin Wilson
All photos copyright 2016 Erin Wilson
Licensed to Jones Kilmartin Group LLC
Unauthorized use prohibited

All content copyright 2016
The Jones Kilmartin Group, LLC
ISBN: 978-1-945817-02-1

Special Thanks to Our Partners

Rachael and Ben Jaffe

Accendo Corporation

Sulaymaniah, Iraq

Erin Wilson, Photographer

Ashna

Bahar

Dyki Zana

Mohammed

Zaneb

Inside

Introduction	6
Meet the Chefs	18
Cooking in Conflict	38
Recipes	44
Recipe Index	110

Introduction

Like many westerners, my understanding of the Iraqi Kurds was shaped by news reporting during my lifetime: their unfortunate geographical location on the border between Iraq and Iran during that war of the 1970s; the horror stories of their own President Saddam Hussein using chemical weapons on them; our government's intervention for them in the form of the "No Fly Zone"; their assistance to the west in overthrowing the despot Hussein.

As my plane began the choppy descent through the blistering heat of early June 2014 into Erbil (aka Hawler), reality began to confront my preconceptions. I expected a beaten down people scurrying in fear through lives of despair and frustration. And little could I have blamed them for that considering all the aggression this people had endured just in my lifetime.

I could not have been more wrong. What short shrift my westerner's myopia gave to a complex, vital people. Here's what my brief week did find and how this book came to be.

The Erbil airport was a modern, brand new concrete, glass and steel beauty offering all the anti terrorism safeguards including remote drop off/pick up terminals. My first encounter with a local was in the ladies room where I garnered some attention due to the "boot" on my sprained foot. A woman approached me and asked, "American?" Through gestures and broken English she inquired as to my pain over a long journey and welcomed me. The government officials running customs/immigration were equally charming and very efficient. It was easier and faster for me to get into Iraq than it was to return to America from Canada in years previous!

Friends met us and transported us from Erbil. The city overall was modern and so very new, like the suburbs of Phoenix or Atlanta. Hardly the bombed out shells of buildings I had expected. These people were on the road to prosperity paved by the oil drilling in the area.

On the road out of town, our local driver explained that we would be taking a less direct route on back roads rather than venture through the somewhat contested Kirkuk area via highway. These roads were isolated save an occasional truck or car generally driven at break neck speed coming or going to the Turkish border north of Erbil.

I tried to wrap my head around being within 100 miles of the Iranian border as we trekked inside the towering Zagros Mountains—the occasionally nebulous border between the two countries. Dusty vistas gave way to a close up tiny village comprised of a few houses and a tiny mosque. This repeated every 20 miles or so.

About an hour in the landscape changed to the beautiful fertile region around Dukan Lake. We passed through a town, replete with roadside sellers of cheap imported toys, and gas stations and a check point. The guards beamed at my US passport and waved us through. I was told these intra-Kurdish checkpoints were designed to weed out Arabs who might be looking to stir up trouble. Thus began my understanding that the Kurds are not Arabs (as us westerners generally lump

all Middle Easterners, save the Jews) and that division fuels much.

As we approached Sulaymaniah the roads became highways with directional signs to Kirkuk, Fallujah and Baghdad. It was quite surreal to see such. My friend explained that modern Suli (as locals refer to it) had modernized and grown really only over the past seven years. People in search of economic and physical

security left those little villages for the opportunity afforded by a growing city. An economic development story played out through history around the world, I recalled from my economics studies.

I spent the next week in my friends' home. It was modern and beautiful, the one vestige of development being the occasional (daily) electricity drop for an hour or so. What jumped out was the food and entertaining which I learned was germane to the region and people. Part of my week was spent touring the region. The open air market stacked with fruits, spices, nuts, hanging meats, and every product imaginable took most of a day before the sandstorm (literally) blew in and sent us scurrying for home laden with bounty.

A highlight was a coffee shop festooned with local artwork (on sale) and relics from the owner's family village. The owner's family, like many, fled or sent their children to Europe—The Netherlands, Belgium, France—during Saddam's reign of terror. These young people have returned determined to reclaim and advance their homeland incorporating this western influence. At night in this same establishment I enjoyed a glass of wine with my companions watching the soccer matches.

There are parks everywhere. The Kurds love parks and children. Children wander unsupervised exploring and playing – yet safe. Ironically, such freedom is unimaginable in the United States. The children are beautiful and curious and hopeful.

My business days were filled with meetings with NGOs and small local businessmen wanting to learn how western small businesses exploit new markets, products and generally grow, because these people are busy building a new economy. Their warmth and hospitality was engulfing. Their focus on learning and planning for their futures stood in stark contrast to the actual current events of those very days.

The day after I arrived in Iraq, an otherwise little known group of terror mongers, ISIL, stormed across the desert. Western news agencies reported the dire news frightening my family in the US—and truthfully, me. But the Kurds did not appear to be frightened. They spoke with pride and confidence of the Peshmerga, their vaunted military which is theirs and not Iraq's (I had the honor of meeting a few of the veterans). In their lifetimes the Peshmerga have fought both alongside and against the Iraqi army.

Theirs is a culture steeped in survival. They've had to be to sustain their autonomous personality over centuries of being under seizure. They figured out early what's important: family and friendship and they've maintained that over dinners and kitchens throughout their history.

I learned these are not a people who become war torn. Rather they are emboldened to build a future of security and economic prosperity for their children. They fiercely embrace family and celebration as they preserve the best parts of a society and history of which they are proud. It's not that they don't understand the awfulness of war and the evils of terrorization (they were, after all, the victims of chemical attack from Saddam Hussein). They face it and yet they also welcome the war displaced.

Even in early June 2014 in Suli alone, they hosted some quarter million refugees from the Iraq war. Since then that number has burgeoned to estimates of over a million refugees displaced from Syria and regions within Iraq.

My final evening in Suli we drove past the new fast food joints, mini golfs and amusement parks, hotels, office buildings and tracts of homes up into the mountains. We were hardly alone, as throngs of picnickers (a family favorite past time especially on Friday afternoons after Mosque services) ascended alongside us. High up we stopped at a lookover. Taking in the growing city below, I gazed across the horizon at the setting sun, Iran behind me, Baghdad southeast and murderous madmen ascending from the northeast.

My week had shown me a fiercely strong people who looked to the future not just with respect for the growing adversity (which the months have shown to be quite real), but with resolve to build a beautiful destiny come what may.

Once back in the US, I followed with concern the movements of ISIL, western, Asian and mid-eastern governments, Syria—the whole boiling pot. I sadly heard my fellow citizens, neighbors and Christians ridiculing and spewing hatred towards the refugees and inhabitants of the Middle East. It would be easy to dismiss them as simply not being enlightened as I (now) was. They knew what media and leaders said.

Who could better show the commonality of the peoples than the Kurds themselves? Thus was born this book. Those same small Kurdish businessmen I had met entered into contracts to provide content for this book both as a business enterprise and as a voice for their people. The faces you see have been compensated and share in the royalties alongside the business entity.

Meet these Kurds—your contemporaries—and hear their stories and values. See how feeding and celebrating with their families is the broadcloth of their lives, as it is in the west. And make some wonderful recipes!

Margaret Jones Kilmartin

Meet the Chefs

Ashna

Ashna

- Favorite foods: yaprakh and red rice
- Ashna learned to cook when she was married, and asked her sister to help teach her, since her family was living with her sister's family at the time.
- "If you serve a nice dinner, everyone comes to the table to share the meal. We spend quality time together. If the food isn't good, everyone goes their own way and I don't see them." She says that her self-confidence has grown since people now know her as a good cook. Ashna also likes how food brings extended family and neighbors together, "It's a good excuse for gathering people."

Dyki Zana

Dyki Zana

- Favorite food: Rice!

- Dyki Zana began learning to cook when she was 16 years old. She learned from her mother. Her favorite memory is when she accidently served salt in the tea she prepared for guests.

- "Can anyone live without food? Food is important to everyone!" She loves cooking for husband and kids. This is one of the ways that she shows love to them.

- Despite the rift between Kurds and Arabs, she and her husband have tried to help Arab displaced families living in their city since the conflict with ISIS began. "Loving always is the most important thing anyone can do!"

Bahar

Bahar

- Favorite foods: Shifta, rice
- Bahar learned to cook right away when she got married, around 24 years old. She learned watching tv and watching others around her.
- Life changed drastically in 2003 when Saddam fell. The economy blossomed and there was financial opportunity for her family. They built their own home together, her husband overseeing the construction and she designing and decorating. "Wherever I am, I love to make things beautiful! I love making things with my own hands in my own way. By doing this, I make it mine!"

Zaneb

- Favorite food: Yaprax, kifta, doina, keshkek (dried yoghurt dish), gippa (sheep intestines stuffed with rice)

- Zaneb was a child when she learned. She learned from her sisters and sister in law. They all lived together in one house so she had many cooks to watch growing up.

- "Nice food makes your heart feel happy. Familiar food brings comfort." "I love having guests, and I want them to feel comfortable when they are in my home." "But I don't have the energy any more to cook like when I was young."

Mohammed

- Favorite foods: Ginger carrot juice for breakfast

- At around age 14 he got his first job and worked at a restaurant. He learned to cook from the chef. Over the next 3 years, he learned the different preparations for dishes served at the restaurant. When he was 17, Mohammed got his first job being head chef and has continued cooking in restaurants for the past 34 years.

- "Because Kurds aren't a patient people. They like to have full bellies. Kurds don't fight, they don't cause trouble, they don't play with technology, they just eat! Since they like to eat, I like to cook!"

Cooking in Conflict

While the Kurds have a long history of being divided like chattel—hence the Iraqi, Turkish, Syrian, Iranian, etc. Kurds, our chefs' lives have been affected by the strife during their lifetimes.

Their parents and grandparents had seen the high point of the overthrow of the Iraqi monarchy in 1958. On the heels of that came an Iraqi constitution which actually recognized and gave rights to the Kurds in Iraq.

The early 1960's saw rebellion and turmoil until the Kurds were recognized as a separate nationality from the Arabs in 1970 and granted autonomy. But that didn't bring peace and prosperity as many had hoped. Rather, civil war ensued between warring political parties: the KDP and the PUK. For many, this period was the most challenging.

Chef Dyki Zana recalls the civil warring period as really hard for her family. There was no electricity. Summers in Iraq see temperatures regularly above 110° Fahrenheit.

No electricity means no cold water to battle these temperatures. She recalls having her children drink from the swamp cooler—the dirty water evaporated by the machine—just to have some refreshment.

Chef Ashna tells of being with her family in a tent quite near the Iranian border in the mid-90's during the civil war. She had worked and made a meal she was proud of, among the best in months. She had spread the plates and food and gathered her family when suddenly "bullets started flying" all around them. She fled with others to hide in the caves in the mountains. She wryly smirks as she states, "We never even got to eat that whole meal."

When the civil clash became intense in Sulaymaniah, Bahar recalls having only bread and dried fruit to provide for her family at every meal.

In 1991 the Kurdish military force—the Peshmerga—began fighting with Saddam Hussein's Iraqi forces. The border between them was fortified by Hussein and an impenetrable blockade was imposed.

According the Chef Ashna's family, "Saddam wouldn't allow a kid carrying a sandwich across the border checkpoints!"

She also emphasized what a tax the Western sanctions on Iraq created for a woman with a family. Rice and beans were a luxury, and most families could only provide two meals a day to their children due to the shortages caused by the sanctions. There was no flour, rice, or sugar. She, and other mothers, substituted in tomatoes, bulgur wheat, soybeans and lentils to feed starving bellies. The chai tea, staple of the Kurdish culture, had to be sweetened with dates.

US led coalition forces invaded Iraq in 2003. The bombing affected areas near the Kurds and led to the Peshmerga joining with the US led coalition and taking control of Mosul and Kirkuk as well as eventually helping topple the Hussein regime.

Zaneb recalls that her family was more fortunate than most during this time of rationing. They had money to buy the rations. Bahar says during conflict times, "We used less of everything." She could only get rice in their

diets twice a week, and she substituted potatoes in for meat in her recipes. The recipes had to be prepared over wood fires, rather than gas, as there was none.

Mohammed also speaks of the challenge of cooking over wood—and the smoke. He made bread using palm flour. He goes on to explain that Kurds prioritize food over other comforts because they remember having very little to eat. He says Kurds eat fast, because they are accustomed to having none.

Kurds are a social society. They are in and out of each others homes. Most kitchens have a futon for visiting. A woman's pride is representing her family as a hostess, which means offering steaming platters of food.

Perhaps most telling of the cultural effect conflict and sanctions have had on the Kurds are these words from Mohammed,

> "When guests came to visit, we had no food to offer, and it was very shameful."

Taskababi

One of the few Kurdish dishes with a spicy kick, this soup wonderfully balances the heat of the chilies and the acidity of the tomato and lemon.

Serves 6

Ingredients

- 1/2 kilogram Bone-in beef
- 1 Large onion
- 2 Chili peppers
- 1 tbsp. Oil
- 3/4 cup Tomato paste
- 1/2 tbsp. Hot paprika
- 1/2 tsp Cinnamon
- 2 Whole dried lemons
- 1 tbsp. Salt

⇒ Cover beef with water in saucepan and simmer for 2 hours or until tender. Set aside.

⇒ Dice onion and saute in oil until translucent. Add spices and cook for 2 more minutes, and then add to pot with beef and broth.

⇒ Reheat soup to a simmer and add tomato paste, stir until dissolved. Add chili peppers and dried lemons.

⇒ Cook on simmer for 15 minutes, and serve with rice.

Recipe from: Mohammed

Recipe from: Bahar

Kulicha

A common companion to a hot cup of chai in any Kurdish house, Kulicha cookies come in two main varieties: date and spiced walnut. The date version resembles a fig netwon though it is much tastier, and the spiced walnut Kulicha are sure to be a winner for your family.

Kulicha

Ingredients

Dough:
- 3 cups Flour
- 1/2 cup Sugar
- 2 tsp Baking powder
- 1 cup Butter
- 2/3 cup Water
- 1 Egg

Filling:
- 1/2 tsp Cardamom
- 1/2 tsp Cinnamon
- 1/2 tsp Anise

AND
- 1 cup Dates

OR
- 1 cup Walnuts
- 1/4 cup Sugar

⇒ Start by adding flour, sugar, and baking powder into a bowl and mixing together. Mix butter and egg in until you have a crumbly mixture. Add 2/3 cup of water until dough comes together. Immediately transfer to a floured surface.

⇒ Preheat the oven to 350 and roll out the dough. For the date cookies, roll the dough into a long narrow shape and add the dates to the surface of the dough. For the walnut cookies, roll out the dough and cut out three inch circles.

⇒ For the date cookies, roll the dough into a log shape, and cut into 1 & 1/2 inch pieces. For the walnut cookies, fill the cookie with the nut mixture, and make sure the mixture is sealed inside the cookie.

⇒ Bake until browned on the top.

Recipe from: Dyki Zana

Mezowra

Mezowra is a light and satisfying tomato based soup. The bitterness of the swiss chard is muted by the acidity of the tomato. The result is a tart, clean-tasting soup that's perfect for a light lunch.

Serves 6

Ingredients
- 1 Medium onion
- 4 cups Swiss chard, washed and chopped
- 2 Garlic cloves
- 1 cup Tomato paste
- 1/2 cup Rice

⇒ Dice onion and saute in a little oil. When the onions are translucent, add in the garlic and swiss chard, and continue to saute for 2-3 minutes.

⇒ Add tomato paste, rice, and 5 cups of water and bring to a boil.

⇒ Put on medium to low flame for 20 minutes until rice is cooked through.

⇒ Serve alone or with bread!

> "I love having guests, and I want them to feel comfortable when they are in my home."
>
> -Zaneb

Mast Aw

You're not in Kurdistan if there's not a big bowl of mast aw in the middle of the dinner spread. This tart yoghurt drink is a good choice if you like savory drinks. It's creamy and not overpowering!

Serves 6

Ingredients

- 4 cups Water
- 2 cups Fresh yoghurt

Mix the two ingredients together until combined and enjoy!

Recipe from: Zaneb

Kabab Makhshi

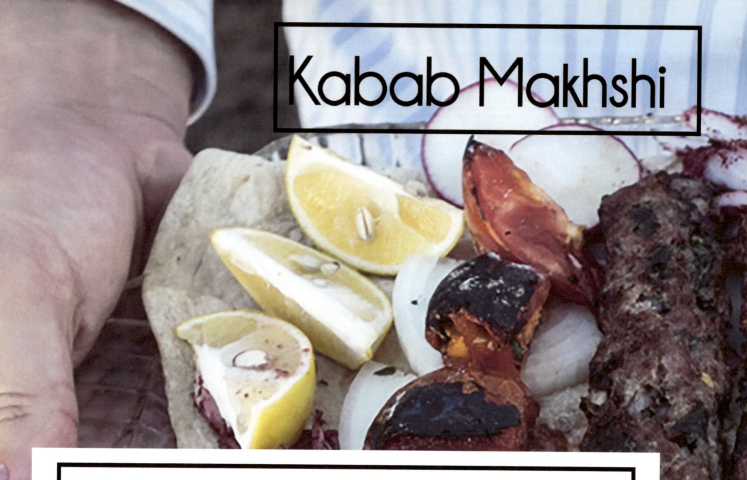

Walk down any busy Kurdish street and you will smell kabab being grilled at a local shop. With picnics so deeply engrained into Kursdish culture, grilling is too. Kurds grill hot and fast, close to the flame. Most Kurds eat kabab sada (plain), but this traditional kabab makhshi recipe is the way to go.
Serves: 6

Ingredients
- 1/2 kilogram Coarse ground beef
- 1/2 kilogram Coarse ground lamb
- 1 Medium onion
- 1 cup Parsley, chopped
- 4 Chilies, minced
- 4 Garlic cloves, minced

Recipe from: Mohammed

- Mix the meat together in a bowl. Have a bowl of water for keeping your hands wet to the side.
- Combine the onion, garlic, chilies, and parsley on a flat plate or tray.
- Make the meat into 2 1/2 inch balls, one for each kabab. Take a ball and distribute the meat along the kabob stick, and then roll in the onion/garlic mixture.
- Prepare charcoal; this should be a hot barbeque because Kurds do not enjoy slow cooking on the grill. Remove grill rack and place kabab as close to the flame as possible. Flip once.
- Enjoy with a piece of naan and grilled tomatoes.

Lamb & Apricot Soup

Kurdish apricot soup, or Qysi, is often served at holiday meals. It's sweet, tangy, and very well balanced.

Serves 6

Ingredients:
- 1/2 kilogram Dried apricots
- 1 tbsp. Vegetable ghee
- 1/2 cup Raisins
- 1/4 kilogram Lamb, bone-in

- Braise the lamb in about 2 inches of water for 1 1/2 hours.
- Put apricots in a saucepan with about three inches of water. Reduce until apricots are soft.
- Add ghee, raisins, and lamb along with the lamb stock that was left. Cover and simmer for a half hour.
- Taste should be a little sweet; add a little sugar if it's too sour.

Recipe from: Zaneb

Garlic Falafel

Common in most Mideast cultures, Mohammed's version of falafel is a nice garlicy twist to the more standard deep-fried chickpea fritters. Mohammed serves this dish with his amba sauce, the salty mustardy taste pairing quite well with the falafel.
Serves 6

Recipe from: Mohammed

Garlic Falafel

Ingredients

Falafel:
- 900 grams Chickpeas, soaked overnight
- 1 Medium tomato
- 1/2 Medium onion
- 4 Garlic cloves
- 1 1/2 tbsp. Chili flakes
- 1 tbsp. Salt

Amba sauce:
- 1/3 cup Amba spice mix (ground mustard, chili powder, paprika, cumin, and turmeric)
- 1/2 Bunch of parsley, chopped
- 1 Clove of garlic, minced

⇒ Start with the falafel. In a food processor or blender, mix all ingredients until everything is combined.

⇒ Begin to heat 3/4 inch of oil in a pan. Using a falafel scoop or spoon, form the batter into falafel shapes, and then immediately place them in the hot oil. Fry until golden brown.

⇒ For the amba sauce, slowly add hot water to the spice mix, making a paste. Stir in the rest of the ingredients, and add red pepper flakes to taste.

⇒ Serve the sauce alongside falafel, meats, and sandwiches

> "Kurds don't fight, they don't cause trouble, they don't play with technology, they just eat! Since they like to eat, I like to cook!
> -Mohammed

Kuba

Kuba is a yellow rice dough stuffed with meat, nuts, raisins and spices and fried golden brown. It can be greasy but is uniquely flavorful.
Serves 6

Recipe from: Mohammed

Kuba

Ingredients

Filling:
- 1/2 kilogram Coarsely ground beef
- 1 Medium onion
- 1/2 Bunch of parsley
- 1/4 cup Yellow raisins
- 1/4 cup Chopped almonds
- 1 tsp Mild curry powder
- 1 tsp Paprika
- 1 tbsp. Salt

Dough:
- 1 cup Short grain rice
- 1 tsp Tumeric
- 1 tbsp. Salt
- 2 Eggs for eggwash

- Start with the filling. Begin by adding oil in a pan and begin browning the meat. Add spices and finely minced onion and cook for 2-3 minutes.
- Add raisins, almonds, parsley, and salt. Stir together and cook for another minute, then set aside.
- To prepare the dough, add rice, salt and turmeric to 3 cups of boiling water and cook until water is completely absorbed. The result will be sticky, starchy rice.*
- Once the rice is no longer too hot to touch, begin kneading the rice together as a dough, dampening with water as needed. Once it has become workable dough, start forming 2 inch balls.**
- Once each ball is formed, flatten it, place meat mixture in the center, and close the dough around it, similar to the shape on an American football.***
- Heat 3/4 of an inch of oil in a pan. Dip kuba one at a time in eggwash and place in hot oil. Do not overcrowd the pan. Fry to a golden color.
- Serve with bread, and sliced tomatoes and parsley.

*Before the assembly of the dough, prepare a bowl of water. This will keep your hands from sticking to the rice dough as you work with it.

**Work quickly, as the rice dries out very quickly.

***As you complete sets of kuba, cover them so they do not dry out.

Kifta

Kifta is the quintessential Kurdish food. A hearty stew with extra-large bulgur wheat balls stuffed with meat, almonds, and raisins. Serves 6

Recipe from: Zaneb

> **"Nice food makes your heart feel happy. Familiar food brings comfort."**
>
> —Zaneb

Kifta

Ingredients

Dough:
- 1/2 kilogram Freshly ground bulgur wheat
- 2 tsp Corn starch
- 1 tbsp. Tomato paste
- 1 tsp Kabab spice (chili powder, sumac, allspice, garlic)

Filling:
- 1/2 kilogram Ground beef
- 1 Large onion
- 1 cup Almonds
- 1 Bunch of parsley
- 1/2 cup Raisins
- 1 tsp Kabab spice

Soup:
- 1/2 kilogram Meat with the bone, cooked
- 1 Large onion
- 1 kilogram Tomato
- 3 tbsp. Tomato paste
- 1 kilogram Swiss chard
- 2 cups Chickpeas

- ⇒ Wash the bulgur and let sit wet for an hour. Add corn starch, tomato paste and spice. Knead mixture until it comes together forming as a dough. Cover and set aside.

- ⇒ For the meat mixture, cook the meat on medium heat. Chop onions and almonds, and add to the meat along with spices. Transfer to a bowl, and add the paste and parsley. Put meat mixture inside dough, forming dumplings.

- ⇒ For the soup, fry the onions and tomatoes. Add 5 liters of water, add swiss chard, chick peas, spice, and salt. Add balls one at a time. Bring soup to a boil, then reduce to a simmer for approximately 1 hour, or until the balls are firm to the touch.

- ⇒ Add kabab spice to the soup to your liking, serve with bread and enjoy!

Ingredients
- 1/2 Chicken, poached
- 2 Medium carrots
- 2 Small potatoes
- 3/4 cup Walnuts, roughly chopped or whole
- 1/4 cup Yellow lentils
- 3/8 cup Raw almonds
- 1/2 cup Raisins
- 150 grams Green peas
- 1/2 cup Tomato paste
- 2 & 1/4 tbsp. Briyani spice
- 3 & 1/4 cups Uncooked rice
- 1/3 cup Oil
- 5 & 1/2 cups Water
- 50 grams Vermicelli
- 1 & 3/4 tbsp. Salt

Recipe from: Ashna

Kurdish Briyani

The Iraqi Kurdish version of Briyani is a nutty and flavorful entrée. Certainly a stand alone dish, Kurds will usually eat it with Fasulya (white bean) soup.
Serves 6

Kurdish Briyani

- Peel and chop carrots and potatoes. Cover a deep frying pan with oil and begin by frying potatoes until almost cooked all the way through and set aside. Repeat with carrots and remove from oil.

- Add half of the briyani spice to hot oil—about a minute, then add cooked chicken to sautee. Follow by adding potatoes, carrots, almonds and walnuts to the mixture. Cook over medium heat for 5 minutes.

- In a separate large pot, pour oil to about 1/4 inch high. Add other half of briyani mix, tumerik, and vermicelli. Fry together until vermicelli is dark brown. At this point add water to the hot oil. When water has come to a boil, add rinsed rice and lentils along with a handful of salt. Keep uncovered until water has evaporated.

- Move pot to a small burner. Make a large hole in the middle of the rice and add the chicken mixture inside and stir together. Cover. Let sit for 20 minutes on low. Stir through and let sit for another 15 minutes.

Enjoy with a crowd!

Ghaful's Salad

A twist on a basic Kurdish salad (tomatoes, cucumber, and lemon), this fresh and tasty salad is named after Ashna's brother-in-law and packs an herby punch.
Serves 6

Ingredients
Salad:
- 4 Medium tomatoes
- 5 Medium cucumbers
- 1 Bundle of mint
- 1 Bundle of parsley
- 1 Bundle of tarragon
- 1/4 cup Cooked chickpeas
- 1 Handful of un-pitted black olives

Dressing:
- 1 tbsp. Olive oil
- 1 tbsp. Pomegranate Syrup
- 1 Lemon, juice and zest

⇒ Finely chop ingredients and mix together with dressing. Enjoy!

Recipe from: Ashna

Recipe from: Zaneb

Shifta

These pan fried flattened meatballs are a nice Kurdish twist when you have grown weary of the same old hamburgers for dinner.

Serves 6

Ingredients
- 1/2 kilogram Ground beef
- 1 cup Bread crumbs
- 1 Large onion
- 1 Bunch of parsley, stems and leaves
- 1 Large head of garlic
- 3 tbsp. Tomato paste
- 1 tsp Shifta spice (cubeb berries, black pepper, nutmeg, chili powder)

⇒ Chop onion, parsley, tarragon, and garlic. Mix with tomato paste and meat. Add spices and bread crumbs to mixture. Mix until it stays together, and won't fall apart when fried.

⇒ Create thin meat patties and place in 1/4 inch of oil to fry. Fry until dark on both sides.

⇒ Serve with French fries, or on sandwiches topped with tomatoes and cucumbers.

Shakiri Qoolaw

These customizable sugars are a classic Kurdish way to enjoy a cup of chai. They are done in a variety of flavors. Next time you have guests, serve these nutty cinnamon sugar cubes with a hot drink to add a Mid-eastern flair!

Recipe from: Bahar

Ingredients
- 1 cup Water
- 3 cups Sugar
- 1 cup Crushed walnuts, or other soft nuts
- 1/2 tsp Cinnamon

⇒ Boil water and sugar on medium heat, and stir gently until the sugar dissolves and the mixture is foaming.

⇒ Take off of heat and continue to stir. Coat a baking sheet with oil and evenly spread crushed walnuts and cinnamon. Pour sugar mixture over walnuts.

⇒ Let sit for 2 hours until hard.

⇒ Turn over onto a wooden surface and cut into small cubes. Serve with tea or coffee.

Sour Egg Soup

Kurds claim this will fix any stomach illness! Try for yourself. In an attempt at full disclosure, this is honestly not the tastiest dish, and certainly not the most beautiful.

Serves 6

Ingredients
- 1 Onion
- 4 Eggs
- 2 cups Water
- 2 tbsp. Oil
- 1-2 tsp Salt
- 1 cup Sumac seeds

⇒ Soak sumac seeds in water. Then, remove and discard the seeds.

⇒ Saute onion in oil until slightly browned. Crack four eggs directly into the onions and stir.

⇒ When eggs are broken up and cooked through, add water from soaked sumac. Add salt to taste.

Recipe from: Zaneb

Recipe from: Ashna

Tirshiat

Pickled Vegetables. You will find these soured pickled vegetables on every Kurdish family's table at almost every meal. It comes in two varieties, yellow and the red one, explained below. People usually just eat a couple bites during the meal for a change in taste.

Ingredients
- 1 Small jar of pickels
- 2 Cucumbers
- 1 Head of garlic
- 1/2 Head of cauliflower
- 1/2 Head of white cabbage
- 1/2 Head of red cabbage
- 1 Beet

⇒ chop cabbage, cauliflower, cucumber, beet, and garlic.
⇒ add whole pickles to the medley.
⇒ add to a tall glass pot or pottery vase and fully cover with red grape vinegar.
⇒ let sit for three days in a warm place. Add hot peppers to taste.

Fasulya Ba Gostawa

South Kurdistan Lamb and beans. Fasulya (white bean) soup is a staple meal in every Kurdish home. Most Kurds will eat this at least 2-3 times a week. Simple, hearty, and the undisputed favorite of all Kurds!
Serves 6-8

Ingredients

- 3 cups Dry white beans
- 1 tbsp.. Salt
- 3 tbsp. Oil
- 1 & 1/2 cups tomato paste
- 1 kilogram Lamb, bone-in

⇒ Pressure cook beans partially ahead of time.

⇒ Sprinkle lamb with salt and brown in a pan. Add 2 inches of water and poach for an hour.

⇒ Add partially cooked beans to a pot along with poached lamb, tomato paste, salt, and oil. Bring to low simmer for about 1 hour.

⇒ Serve with rice and a piece of naan.

Recipe from: Ashna

Recipe from: Ashna

Sheikh Makhshi

A delightful named after a Sheikh who apparently liked things makhshi (stuffed). Garden veggies stuffed with a slightly sweet meat mixture. It's rich without being heavy.

Serves 6

Ingredients
- 1 kilogram Ground beef
- 1 kilogram Eggplant
- 1 kilogram Zucchini
- 4 Green peppers
- 4 Medium potatoes
- 4 Medium onions
- 1 & 1/2 cup Tomato paste
- 2 Large bundles of parsley
- 1/3 cup Red lentils
- 1/2 cup Raw almonds
- 1 cup Walnuts
- 1 cup Raisins

Sheikh Makhshi

- Salt ground beef and cook on medium heat as not to dry it out. Add some water at the end to keep meat moist. Add chopped onions and parsley along with raisins, nuts, and lentils. Mix everything together.

- Add 1/2 cup of the tomato paste and 1/2 cup of water. Cook on medium/low heat for 20 minutes.

- Take the zucchini and eggplant and cut in halves or thirds widthwise (or depending on size). Peel, remove part of the centers of the eggplant, zucchini, and potato. Next, lightly fry these along with the peppers on all sides, then let cool on a plate.

- Stuff all of the vegetables with the meat mixture and place carefully in the pot. Put zucchinis and eggplants back together, with the ends and tops back on to make it whole again. This will keep the mixture from leaking back out during the cooking process. Add any remaining meat mixture directly on top of the vegetables. Add 1 cup of tomato paste and a tsp of salt to a liter or so of hot water until paste is dissolved. Pour sauce onto stuffed veggies.

- Cover and place on low simmer for about an hour until liquid has condensed a bit and you have a rich-looking tomato sauce.

Recipe from: Bahar

Pomegranate Molasses

A staple in every Kurdish kitchen, pomegranate molasses is commonly utilized in many Kurdish dishes and salads. This sweet and sour syrup is also delicious over French toast, ice cream, or in a cocktail.

Ingredients
- 10 Pomegranates

⇒ Blend pomegranate seeds in a blender. Pour through a fine strainer until only juice remains.
⇒ Bring to a simmer. Repeatedly remove foam as many times as necessary.
⇒ Reduce on low heat for 1-4 hours, depending on the desired thickness. You can even simmer for up to 8 hours if you want it to become a paste.

Recipe from: Bahar

Yaprakh

Reminiscent of Greek or Turkish dolma, Yaprakh is beautiful vegetable medley stuffed with seasoned rice. It is definitely a go to dish if you are looking to impress guests. It is time consuming and challenging to get perfect the first time, but totally worth it!

Serves 6

Ingredients
- 1/2 kilogram Swiss chard
- 1/2 kilogram Onion
- 2 Small tomatoes
- 2 Zucchini
- 4 Small eggplants
- 2 Small bell peppers
- 3 Potatoes
- 200 grams Parsley
- 1/2 Bone-in chicken, cut in pieces
- 2 & 1/2 cups Rice
- 2 tsp Yaprax spice mix
- 2 tbsp. Tomato paste
- 1 tbsp. Salt
- 1 tbsp. Citric acid

Yaprakh

⇒ Begin by cooking chicken pieces in roughly 2 inches of water until chicken is cooked through and tender, roughly 40 minutes. This step is perfect to do a day ahead of time and put in the fridge until you are ready to simply add it in at the right time.

⇒ Chop parsley and onions and put together with un-cooked rice and tomato paste. Add salt and spice. Take potatoes and cut into round slices. Lightly fry and set aside. You do not cook the potatoes fully.

⇒ Take the pepper, eggplant, zucchini. Depending on how big they are you may need to cut them in half or thirds to make about three inch pieces. Cut the end off and carefully hollow out the inside. Do not discard the end—you will use it later as a lid. Then take the pieces and slightly fry them on all sides until slightly browned.

⇒ Take all of the veggies that you have fried along with the swiss chard and prepare to stuff. Begin lining the bottom of a large pot with the stems of the swiss chard. Follow with the sliced potatoes. Place your prepared chicken pieces on top of the potatoes. Continue by stuffing the onions, eggplant, tomato, pepper, and zucchini with the rice mixture. Top with the stuffed swiss chard covering the top. Only stuff veggies 2/3rds full as the rice will grow as it cooks. Top each piece with the end that you cut off earlier to keep the stuffing in.

- ⇒ To the top of the ensemble, add some of the fat/stock from the chicken you cooked earlier for taste—about 1 cup.
- ⇒ Cover with water until it almost reaches the top of the veggies—about an inch below. Place a heavy plate to add weight and cover veggies. Set on a high flame until you hear it boil. Reduce it to a low flame and leave for an hour. It is done when there is no remaining water in pot.
- ⇒ To serve, remove lid and place a large and round serving dish on top. Flip the entire pot directly onto the serving dish. Place in center of table and serve family style with bread.

Tepsi

Tepsi is a layered vegetable entrée that is both beautiful and delicious. Many Kurds will add beef or lamb, but the vegetarian variety doesn't disappoint. It is so rich and satisfying!

Serves 6

Ingredients
- 1 kilogram Eggplant
- 3 Medium onions
- 1/2 kilogram Tomatoes
- 2 Peppers
- 150 grams Chopped parsley
- 1 & 1/2 tsp Crushed caraway seeds
- 1 tsp Kabab spice
- 1/2 tsp Cumin
- 3 tbsp. Tomato paste

⇒ Cut eggplant into long slices. Cover with salt until they sweat on both sides and wipe the liquid off (this will get the bitterness off). Slice tomatoes, peppers, and onions. Chop parsley and set aside.

⇒ Take the eggplant and cover each slice in flour to prevent eggplant from soaking up too much oil. Let them sit in flour for 10 minutes. Fry eggplant, onion, and pepper slices.

Recipe from: Bahar

⇒ Layer in a pan, starting with tomatoes on the bottom, followed with one layer of eggplant. Here, add the spices, salt, and half of the parsley. Finish with the rest of the eggplant and peppers.

⇒ Add a little water to the tomato paste to make a thick sauce and then dollop on top of the layered vegetables and cover with parsley.

⇒ Put on medium heat until simmering. Cover and reduce heat to a low simmer until the water is nearly gone.

⇒ Remove from heat and let sit for a few minutes. Enjoy!

Recipe from: Bahar

Nut-raisin Topping

Spruce up boring white rice with this tasty and colorful topping. Whether entertaining guests or just trying to make dinner special, Kurds will often add this to steamed rice to make an impression.

Ingredients
- 1/2 cup Raisins
- 1 cup Walnuts
- 1 cup Almonds
- 1 tsp Saffron

⇒ Soak saffron in 1/3 cup water.
⇒ Fry walnuts, almonds and raisins separately.
⇒ Combine nuts and raisins together and top a serving dish of steamed rice with the mixture. Drizzle saffron water on rice for color.

Recipe from: Dyki Zana

Hawler Doina

Doina is a simple 3 ingredient dish similar in texture to grits or cream of wheat. However, don't expect a mild flavor from this traditional Kurdish food. It can pack a savory sour punch! Kurds make doina several different ways. This variety from the city of Hawler (the Kurdish name of the capital Erbil) is eaten as a soup. Many Kurds also make a dried doina which resembles cookies or crackers and traditionally would take them on hunting trips into the mountains.

Ingredients
- 1 liter Yoghurt whey
- 1 cup Cracked bulgur wheat
- 2 tsp Salt

⇒ Bring the whey and salt to a boil in a sauce pan. Add bulgur and reduce to a low simmer for about ten minutes.

⇒ Place the pan on a diffuser for another ten minutes. When the bulgur is soft, it is ready to serve.

Steamed Red Bulgur

Kurds nowadays eat rice for 2 or even 3 meals a day. However, in the 90's, during times of sanctions and war, Kurds ate "sawar," or bulgur wheat, because it was cheaper and grown locally.
Serves 6

Ingredients
- 1 Medium onion
- 1 Clove of garlic
- 1/2 cup Tomato paste
- 2 cups Bulgur wheat
- 1 tbsp. Salt

⇒ Begin by sautéing the onion until translucent.
⇒ Add in the garlic and tomato paste and cook together for about two minutes.
⇒ Add 3 cups of water and bring to a boil.
⇒ Add bulgur and simmer for 20 minutes or until bulgur is tender.

Recipe from: Dyki Zana

Recipe from: Dyki Zana

Qorrow

"Qorrow" literally means muddy water. This is a fitting name for this thick, creamy, and tart stew. Traditionally cooked with mutton or lamb and sheep yoghurt, you can substitute beef and cow's yoghurt if you prefer a less gamey taste.

Ingredients

- 1 kilogram
  Lamb or mutton, bone-in
- 2 cups
  Purslane, washed and chopped
- 3 cups
  Sheep yoghurt

- Braise lamb (or mutton) over low boil in 2 inches of water for about 2 hours.
- Add sheep yoghurt to the meat and stock, and then add the purslane and stir everything together.
- Continue to stir until the soup no longer looks curdled, and instead more blended.
- Add salt to taste and serve.

Lentil & Wild Purslane Soup

This smooth, earthy tasting soup pairs red lentils with wild purslane greens. Most Kurds either find purslane in the mountains or source them out of their gardens.
Serves 6

Recipe from: Dyki Zana

Lentil & Wild Purslane Soup

Ingredients
- 2 cups Red lentils
- 1/2 kilogram Purslane
- 1/2 cup Tomato paste
- 1 Medium onion
- 1 cup Water

⇒ Wash and chop stems and leaves of purslane. Dice onion and sauté with oil until translucent.

⇒ Add the purslane greens to the onions, and add salt and pepper to taste. Continue to cook for 2-3 minutes.

⇒ Add tomato paste along with a cup of water.

⇒ Finish by adding the lentils and additional salt, and simmer until lentils are fully cooked through, about 20 minutes. Serve with bread.

List of Recipes

Fasulya Ba Gostawa	84
Garlic Falafel	58
Ghaful's Salad	74
Hawler Doina	100
Kabab Makhshi	54
Kifta	66
Kuba	62
Kulicha	46
Kurdish Briyani	70
Lamb & Apricot Soup	56
Lentil & Wild Purslane Soup	106
Mast Aw	52
Mezowra	50
Nut-Raisin Topping	98
Pomegranate Molasses	90
Qorrow	104

List of Recipes

Shakiri Qoolaw	78
Sheikh Makhshi	86
Shifta	76
Sour Egg Soup	80
Steamed Red Bulgur	102
Taskababi	44
Tepsi	96
Tirshiat	82
Yaprakh	92

CPSIA information can be obtained
at www.ICGtesting.com
Printed in the USA
LVHW071006151121
703373LV00002B/25